THINKING MATTERS

CHARLES MERRETT

MINDS EYE BOOKS

THINKING MATTERS *is based on extracts from;*

A GUIDE TO EXPERIENCE

published by MINDS EYE BOOKS 2001
16 Helena Road, Southsea, Hants, PO4 9RH, England
Tel; 02392 831457

copyright Charles Merrett 2001

All rights reserved. No part of this publication may be reproduced or transmitted, in any form or by any means, without permission.

ISBN 1-873828-02-0

This book is sold subject to the condition that it shall not, by way of trade or otherwise, be lent, re-sold, hired out, or otherwise circulated without the publisher's prior consent in any form of binding or cover other than that in which it is published and without a similar condition including this condition being imposed on the subsequent purchaser.

Acknowledgements

This book would not have been possible without the patient support of my wife and companion Christina. I am also grateful to two psychologist colleagues, Sylvia Weaver and Simon Easton, for reading the manuscript and for their helpful discussions over many years.

Special thanks are due to Homer Maladroit for the use of his quotations.

Charles Merrett
Southsea, May 2001

The Author;
Charles Merrett MA(Cantab), Dip Psych, has worked as a Clinical Psychologist for 25 years. He is married with four children.

on thinking and being;

"I think, therefore I am."
RENE DESCARTES

"I am, therefore I think"
HOMER MALADROIT

two views of thinking

**"The happiest life
is to be without thought."**
SOPHOCLES

**"The unexamined life
is not worth living."**
SOCRATES

INTRODUCTION

This book is about thinking; more particularly about the important part our thinking plays in our feelings and experience. It argues that the ideas we currently use to understand feelings and experience are inadequate; inadequate because they imply we are helpless victims of our nature and circumstances, and because they give rise to many of our psychological problems. The book then offers a way of thinking about experience that can transform our ability to understand ourselves and to manage our lives more effectively.

Traditionally, we have come to regard thinking as the logical, rational, (even cold), process by which we make sense of the world. In this sense we have come to see thinking and emotion as opposites, or at least as if they are quite different processes. We even locate them differently within us when we say we think with our heads, and feel with our hearts.

Perhaps, this identification of thinking with rationality has come about partly because of the astonishing success of 'rational' thinking within the sciences and technologies. But this is a restricted use of the word *thinking* and one that fails to recognise the importance of other sorts of thinking.

In the present book *thinking* is taken to include all of the different sorts and levels of mental processing we are capable of. In this sense thinking underpins everything we do. Thinking ranges from ideas about how things in the world work, to how we would like them to be; from scientific theories to religious beliefs; from technologies to fashion; from international co-operation to genocide; from great works of art to a child's stick figure; from love to hate; from self-sacrifice to greed; from a kindly gesture to turning one's back. All of these activities depend on our thinking.

It is thinking in its detail and complexity that distinguishes the human species from others; one person from another; and, perhaps less obviously, one experience from another.

So in this book we will conceive of thinking very broadly; not just as an attempt to understand the world as it is; nor as simply the means by which we undertake the practical tasks of our lives. While these are impressive enough aspects of thinking, when we think we are doing something else; something equally subtle and powerful.

When we think we are also imposing on the world our view of what we like and dislike; what we want and fear; what we feel the world should be like and what we hope it is not; what we think is important and what we think is not.

These acts of thinking are, of course, subjective and personal rather than rational; but more importantly they are evaluative. They are based on values; that is they are not determined by the way things are in themselves, but they reflect human will and choices between ranges of options.

When these values are shared between large groups of people they are the stuff of social progress, art, fashion; or of politics, international conflict, and racism. On a more local level they are the stuff of membership, neighbourhood, collaboration; or of mobs, vandalism, and ostracism.

On an interpersonal level values are the stuff of relationship, sharing, support; or of rivalry, jealousy and criticism.

Our evaluative thinking is not separate and distinct from our rational scientific thinking. The two are interwoven inextricably, seamlessly. Even the history of science, which we have come to assume is a triumph of impersonal human rationality over nature, is a very human history, littered with examples of individual's personal values, hopes and petty jealousies that shape the development of the science.

If this is the case in the realms of scientific thinking it is even more so in our everyday lives. In this arena our personal values, hopes, fears, ambitions, jealousies, plans are centre stage, and for most of us our rational, scientific thinking plays at best a minor walk-on part.

Our personal values become the very framework not just of our lives, but of each of our experiences.

on the influence upon us of our thoughts;

"There is nothing either good or bad, but thinking makes it so."
SHAKESPEARE, Hamlet

"Men are not disturbed by things, but by the opinions they make of them…When we are impeded or disturbed by others let us never blame others, but ourselves, that is, our opinions."
EPICTETUS

"Do not distress yourself with imaginings."
MAX EHRMANN

"Mark your unhappiness with balanced words; do not inflame it with immoderate names."
HOMER MALADROIT

"Think no more; 'tis only thinking lays lads underground."
A E HOUSEMAN

"Man is the only animal that laughs and weeps; for he is the only animal that is struck with the difference between what things are and what they ought to be."
HAZLITT

"Experience is the child of thought."
DISRAELI

OUR CURRENT WAYS OF THINKING ABOUT EXPERIENCE

Thinking about facts and thinking about values, together these define the human spirit. However, currently we do not take this into account in the way we think about ourselves. In particular, we do not take it into account when we think about the nature of experience; ie, when we think about how our feelings work. (What causes them; what determines their intensity; why they might endure; why they change; what we might do with unwanted feelings.)

While we may recognise the sentiments expressed by the quotations on the previous page, most of us do not live by them in our daily lives. We may intellectually agree with the importance they place on thinking but typically we do not consistently apply them to the detail of our daily lives.

In talking about our feelings, it is very rare that we mention our thinking as something we are doing, and as a cause of our feelings or experience.

In our everyday ways of talking about our feelings we tend to describe ourselves in quite different ways. We tend to see ourselves as pushed and pulled by things that happen around us; by the things people do and say to us and about us; by the 'stress we are under' or by the good things that make us feel 'on top of the world'.

When the things that happen are 'bad' we 'suffer' and it seems that our 'suffering' is inevitable. It seems that it is caused simply and directly by the conditions under which we live, and the events that happen around us. When the things that happen are 'good' we see ourselves as happy.

Then it seems that our pleasure is equally inevitable, and is caused simply and directly by our good fortune or success.

Generally we talk about our feelings as if they are caused by the situations and circumstances of our lives in a direct and mechanistic way.

This view sees us as relatively passive, and even, at times, as the helpless victims of our circumstances.

This is the view we predominantly take nowadays. It is the model that we use in our everyday conversations with each other. It is the model we will read about in newspapers and magazines. It is the model we see in TV programmes and films. In particular, it is the model that is used in much advertising since it allows a product to be represented as the thing that will inevitably solve our problems or bring us happiness.

In short, this way of thinking about experience has come to be the culturally dominant model through which we see ourselves.

This book aims to show that this model is only one way of looking at ourselves and how experience works. It then offers an alternative; an alternative that is apparently simple but that helps us look at ourselves afresh; a model that can have far-reaching consequences for many aspects of our lives.

SOME PROBLEMS WITH OUR CURRENT WAY OF THINKING ABOUT EXPERIENCE

First of all it will be helpful to consider what, if any, are the inadequacies or dangers in our current way of thinking about experience.

Some important consequences seem to flow logically from the idea that our feelings are caused by the situations and circumstances of our lives. This logical flow from one idea to the next may not stand up to critical examination, but this does not really matter. Our everyday conceptions about ourselves are not usually well worked out consistent philosophies (nor do they need to be). What is important is which ideas people actually use in their day-to-day descriptions and what implications these ideas have.

What ideas seem to flow from the notion that our experience in a situation is caused by that situation? How do these ideas shape our experience, our possibilities and limitations?

Presumably, if we take this view of experience, then our role in organising our lives will be to manage what happens to us. Once confronted by something happening to us there is apparently not much we can do about it; we passively suffer the bad and enjoy the good. Therefore, on the whole, our aim should be to avoid bad things and seek out good ones.

We would then have a strong interest in making a map of the world and learning which situations are good and which are bad. We would be assuming that things are either good or bad in themselves, and that this goodness or badness, being a property of the situation or happening, does not change.

But how would we then explain the common observation that different people have different experiences when faced with the same situation?

Perhaps, this does not present too much of a problem. We can simply draw on the idea that people are different. We can assume they have different qualities or tendencies, different personalities. The fact that two people have different experiences when confronted by the same event could then be assumed to be due to these sorts of differences.

We are also likely to assume that these qualities or tendencies are fixed and permanent aspects of the person.

What then if an individual happens to show a particular reaction that is unusual, distressing, or troublesome to themselves or others?

Pursuing the line of thinking we have started, perhaps, such an experience would need to be attributed to some sort of peculiarity, or problem located in the person. If the difficult experience is especially unusual or extreme then we might assume it arises because of a disorder or an abnormality that the person has.

If the difficult experience is short-lived or episodic then we might explain it in terms of the person losing control, 'losing it', becoming 'unstable', 'unhinged' or having a 'break-down'.

All of these suggest that the person has slipped into some temporary state. However, because of the stigma associated with these sorts of explanations we might easily think that, although temporary, their distress reveals something more fundamental and permanent about them as a person. Perhaps, these troublesome experiences are due to the person being 'a bit strange', 'different', 'abnormal'; perhaps, they reveal that they have 'a weak character', are of 'a nervous disposition', or are in some way 'disturbed', have a 'mental illness' or are 'mad'.

From the above we can see that the view that our feelings are caused by the situation is closely linked (at least in practice) with the idea that people are different because they have different fixed qualities, and tendencies; and that problem experiences are caused by abnormalities in the person.

Our ideas about people being different have become so commonplace and familiar that it may, at first, seem totally ridiculous to question them. But as we will see later, the detail of the way in which we assume people are different is actually very important.

Our current ways of thinking about experience attribute two individual's different experiences to differences between them. These differences are assumed to lie inside them in a fixed and more or less permanent way. While we cannot go as far as to argue that people are the same, or potentially the same, we will see that our current ways of thinking about experience have exaggerated the apparent differences between people. If we use a different way of understanding how our feelings arise, we will see that we are potentially more similar to each other than we currently assume.

on words and thinking;

"We dissect nature along lines laid down by our native language. Language is not simply a reporting device for experience but a defining framework for it."
BENJAMIN WHORF

"Take care which words you use to frame any experience, (or even the idea of experience itself) lest they prove to be an invisible cage."
HOMER MALADROIT

"How can I know what I think till I see what I say?"
WALLAS GRAHAM

"Words are meant to convey thought: If you take trouble in the use of words you are bound to clarify the thought you wish to convey."
ANONYMOUS DIPLOMAT

OUR CURRENT IDEAS OF WHY PEOPLE ARE DIFFERENT

Having described briefly how we tend to attribute people's different experiences to different qualities and tendencies, this leads us naturally to the further question of how these differences and abnormalities arise.

Nowadays, there are four main contenders for answers to this question; the individual's biochemistry, their early childhood, their inherited personality (the genetics of behaviour), and their experience of bad events or trauma.

These factors are sometimes seen as competing alternatives but often our explanations use a combination of two or more of them, usually in a loose and undefined way.

These four main candidates for causes are clearly not just part of our everyday ways of thinking but are also prevalent ideas in various professional and academic circles.

There are other factors that have been entertained as possible causes for our differences and particularly our psychological problems. Such things as a blow on the head, the influence of the moon, evil spirits etc. While these are fascinating and tell us a lot about human culture there is not room to explore them here. However, it is worth noting that they share a general characteristic with the above four candidates; they are all external causes which 'happen' to the person and which the latter has little responsibility for and control over.

ARE OUR BIOGRAPHIES CAUSES OF OUR DIFFERENCES?

We can use the term biographies to cover any influences from our life-stories. In practice there are two main issues that we tend to consider; early childhood, and bad events and traumas.

If we react differently to the situations and circumstances of our lives because of differences in our biographies, we might suppose that, if we are particularly distressed or have psychological problems, it must be because we have a damaged or abnormal biography.

We would see the abnormality as being caused by some traumatic event or difficult relationship in the past. We would assume this must be represented in us in a deep and complex way. We might assume that it is more or less fixed in us and that it is always likely to have an effect on us. If our distress has only come to light recently we would assume that the effect of our damaged biography had been lying dormant within us, stalking us, waiting for its time.

If we see things in this way we are likely to predict that change will be very difficult, if not impossible. We will then believe that we need to develop complex technologies for change; forms of therapy that one person can attempt to do to and for another. An initial focus for such therapies would be to identify the sort of bad events and relationships that lead to problems; to answer the question "Why am I like this? Why has this happened to me?".

What might have to follow is an attempt by the therapist to persuade the individual that they did in fact feel badly about the event/relationship identified by the therapist, even though the individual may previously have not recognised its effect. If they had not recognised it they might be supposed, not merely to have not recognised it or forgotten it, but to have repressed it. If the therapist believes in the causal nature of past events and relationships they will often spend an immense amount of time trawling the individual's account of the past looking for potential causes. Then the individual's memory of these will need to be elaborated and reconstructed so that they agree to see them as the cause of the difficulties they are seeking help for.

As therapy and counselling services have expanded, many people have sought help in the belief that they need to discover what it was in their past that has made them so unhappy.

Through these processes people become patients who 'have' problems, and 'receive' or 'undergo' treatment.

A large number of theories from different perspectives have developed to explain people's problems. These have led to a vast range of techniques aimed at helping people overcome their problems. A flourishing industry of helping has resulted. This industry has not been without its critics.

Some of these critics argue that the distressed person comes to see themselves as a victim of their past. In the process their distress can be transformed into anger or despair and sometimes their unhappiness is thereby intensified.

On the pain of thinking

"A moment's thought would have shown him. But a moment is a long time and thought is a painful process."
A E HOUSEMAN

"Many people would sooner die than think. In fact they do."
BERTRAND RUSSELL

"Could one learn to walk without painful collisions with unyielding and stubborn objects? Should one expect to understand without moments of painful confusion"
HOMER MALADROIT

ARE OUR BIOLOGIES CAUSES OF OUR DIFFERENCES?

An alternative explanation to the one that holds that our different experiences are caused by our different biographies or life-stories is that such differences arise because of differences in our biology.

If this were the case we would suppose that particularly bad or difficult experiences must flow from damaged or abnormal biologies; these could be inherited or genetic behavioural tendencies or disturbances in the body's, and especially the brain's, chemistry.

Currently, disordered brain chemistry is, perhaps, the most commonly used biological explanation of difficult experiences.

If a disordered biology is the cause of an individual's problematic reactions to situations, then we will again see the fault or abnormality as lying inside the person, in a way for which the person has little responsibility and can do little about.

The case for disordered biology as a cause may appear strong because, when seen from the outside and from a biological or medical perspective, many difficult experiences we have can appear surprising, complex and even frightening. Furthermore, difficult psychological experiences are not 'all in the mind' but also often have strong physical effects. From a medical viewpoint these physical aspects of bad psychological experiences will be regarded as symptoms. This carries the strong implication that they are symptoms of some sort of illness process occurring within us. Simply using the word 'symptom' to describe parts of our experience conjures up an image of an underlying biological process unfolding within us and marching to its own beat.

Most people consulting a doctor nowadays for complaints involving unhappiness are told they are depressed. The model they are usually offered to explain their feelings is that their depression is caused by a chemical imbalance in their brain.

(Interestingly for those who would claim that this sort of medical diagnosis is a valid scientific tool, the diagnoses of exactly the same complaints some years ago would have been various forms of anxiety related 'disorders'. There are interesting reasons why this change has occurred.)

Clearly the explanation that our unhappiness <u>is</u> depression and that our difficulties arise from a chemical imbalance in our brain, leads logically and incontrovertibly towards attempting to restore our chemical balance with one of the many anti-depressants that are now available on the market.

This way of understanding and dealing with unhappiness has become very widespread. So much so that none of us are now immune from its influence. In practice, (though this is not a logically necessary connection), it is often combined with the assumption that the bad feelings of depression have been triggered by bad things happening to us. Perhaps, two causes are better than one. Both carry the same message that our bad feelings happen to us, and that we are not responsible for them. While this might relieve us from any sense of guilt for how we are feeling, it also disempowers us since, from this perspective, there is little we can do ourselves about our brain chemistry (since we have only limited ways of influencing it), or our pasts (since they are a fait accompli). We become helpless victims twice over.

If bad or distressing feelings arise because of disordered brain chemistry, what implications are there, if any, for what we should do about any lack of positive experiences in our lives?

If we see ourselves as biological machines then we can change the way the machine works by taking a drug to alter its biological processes. We can do this to overcome problem experiences. But by the same logic, why should we not take something to provide or enhance good experiences?

To achieve this we will need to consult a different sort of professional, operating in a far less regulated market; or at least one regulated by different more sinister forces. What these professionals, the dealers and traffickers, can prescribe are often referred to euphemistically as recreational drugs. This term sadly reveals what we currently understand about how experience (in this case happiness) works.

The above suggests that the way we now think about how our feelings work supports the use of recreational drugs. It seems inevitable that society will always have a drug problem while we continue to believe that experience is caused directly by what is in the world around us, and that the differences between people lie in their biographies and especially their biologies.

A DIFFERENT WAY OF THINKING ABOUT EXPERIENCE

From the above we can see that the way we usually think about how our feelings work does have specific and very important implications for how we think about ourselves, how we describe and understand our difficulties, and the possibility of managing our lives, and of change.

We can see that our current ideas about our feelings generally see the individual as the passive victim of biographical and biological forces. These forces are seen as determining the quality of an individual's particular feelings and especially their difficulties. The individual is seen as having qualities and tendencies that are viewed as determined, static, deep-rooted, and not easily changed. These sorts of explanations are, in their style, like those in the natural sciences; they treat human beings and their experience as if they are governed by rational universal laws that are simply 'out there' waiting to be discovered.

Let me offer an example that suggests that there is an alternative and that we should think about experience in a completely different way; a way that is more in keeping with the quotations on page 12.

The example describes a very ordinary activity, but is about the importance of thinking. It highlights various things we do when we think. It shows that these are particularly important if we are to understand the nature and qualities of any of our experiences.

The example shows that all human experience is driven by our evaluative thinking; it is, therefore, a creative expressive process and is not determined by universal laws that are open to mere discovery.

THE DECORATED ROOM

Imagine you are decorating a room. By the time you finish your work you will have been over every square inch of the room. You will know the room in intimate detail. In particular, you will be familiar with all of its imperfections. For example, you will know all of the lumps and bumps in the wall and the woodwork; you will know where the wallpaper refused to fold neatly around a corner or where its pattern insisted on not matching; you will know where your scissors failed to follow the straight line on the skirting board; where each unsteadiness of your hand seemed exaggerated by the lurch of the scissors and was captured forever for all to see.

When you have cleaned up, packed away the decorating equipment and you sit in the room you can allow your eye to be drawn to the imperfections. But in thinking about these things you can take your thinking further and see them not just as imperfections, but you can judge them as mistakes and failures on your part.

You can then develop your thinking further and use this judgement as evidence that you have not done a good job. You can draw the conclusion that you hurried the job and that it looks messy.

You may then remember other decorating jobs that have turned out similarly. You can then take your thinking further and draw the bigger conclusion that you are generally not careful enough and that you are not really a good decorator.

But you can take your thinking even further and conclude that not only are you no good as a decorator but that you are not a very practical person. Everything you do is flawed in some way. It is not as good as it should be.

You can go further still and draw a mega-conclusion that as a person you are as much a disaster as your room.

If you sit in your room and you do this sort of thinking, if you follow this pathway of thinking, you can see that you will feel miserable; miserable not just about the Decorated Room but about yourself and, perhaps, even life itself.

Now another way of looking at the same Decorated Room, is to look at it as a friend would look at it coming into it for the first time.

They would not see the fine detail of the room. They would not see the imperfections. Instead they would see more global aspects of the room. They would see the overall effect; the clean fresh look compared with the tired, perhaps, scruffy room they had last seen. They might see the pattern on the paper, the colour scheme, and the way the room is laid out.

If you, like your friend, were to focus on these elements of the room you might go on to judge them as reasonable or even good. You might then use this as evidence to conclude that you have done a reasonable or even a good job.

You might then take your thinking further and remember other decorating tasks you have done in the past. You might judge that they turned out well and conclude that you are a good decorator.

You might go further still to a bigger conclusion and decide that you are quite a practical person.

Finally you might conclude that you are generally a good person and one you would consider it a privilege to meet.

If you sit in your room and follow this pathway of thinking, then you will feel good not only about the room but about yourself and even life itself; you will feel the opposite of the feelings that you would have if your thoughts followed the first pathway outlined above.

Now it seems that we have discovered something very important in this simple example; we can have two opposite sets of feelings in exactly the same room. We must conclude, therefore, that the room and the way it is decorated does not determine our feelings. The room is actually neutral. The room is the room is the room. The room simply does not mind how we look at it. It does nothing to us to make us look at it in one way or another. It is us that does the looking. It is us that looks at the room in one way or another. It is us that follows a particular pathway of thinking as we sit there.

It is us that creates the pathway of thinking, and this is what determines how we feel as we sit in our room.

Which view we take of the room will determine whether we feel frustrated or satisfied.

If we look at the two views of the room I have described we can see that each point of view is made up of three important sorts of thinking.

FOCUSING

Firstly there is the question of what we select to focus on in any situation.

We cannot absorb everything about a situation in one simple lump. Which aspects do we focus on? Do we focus on the imperfections or the ways in which the room has been improved? Do we focus on the detail or a broader view?

We are a highly selecting animal.

We are not simply and directly in contact with the totality of even our immediate surroundings. We use our senses to find out what is happening around us, but each of these senses is limited so that we can only be aware of a small range of the physical world around us.

Each of our senses also operates in a very selective way. For example, we use our highly developed central vision to get very detailed visual information about that part of our surroundings that our eyes focus on. We use our ears to locate sounds and attend to those that have meaning for us; and to filter out other noises.

The fact that our senses are constructed to allow us to focus them on particular aspects of our world means that we can derive much more detailed information from parts of our surroundings.

They are constructed so that we respond automatically to biologically important aspects of our surroundings, eg, fast movement or sudden noises. However we also learn to tune each of them in to what is of interest or importance to us. We can do this deliberately but we don't have to; it largely happens at an unconscious level as soon as we have made something interesting, relevant or important to ourselves.

A simple example of this is the way we are able to hear our own name more easily than other words when it is spoken in a noisy environment like a crowded room.

If each of our senses is selective we can further select by choosing which of our senses to attend to at any one time. We can, of course, choose not to attend to any of our senses but to concentrate on our inner thoughts, daydreams or worries.

When we are challenged by feelings that are novel, intense or unexpected we can spend a great deal of time focused on them. This inner focus and the pathways of thinking that we generate in our attempts to understand our feelings are often a central part of our psychological problems.

At any point in time we are at best focused on only a small part of what is happening around us. To focus on one thing we must necessarily ignore others, so when we focus we also ignore.

on focusing:

"The mind, like the telescope, is always focused; but it remains useless until someone points it in a chosen direction."
HOMER MALADROIT

"Everything is too complicated for men to be able to comprehend."
ECCLESIASTES

"The focus of our mind is infinitesimal and in each moment we face an infinity of choice."
HOMER MALADROIT

JUDGING

The second important part of the thinking we do in the Decorated Room is that having focused on something we then judge it.

For example, we turn neutral imperfections into mistakes and failings with the power to intimidate and embarrass; or we turn other aspects into improvements with the power to please and impress.

This power, of course, does not come from the imperfections or improvements but from our judgements of them.

Just as we are a very selective animal we seem to be a very judgmental animal .

We can hardly consider anything without also deciding (or in actuality choosing) whether it is good or bad, weak or strong; whether we like it or dislike it. We constantly compare one thing with another; assert which one is better; which looks good; which is good or bad style.

Similarly we set standards of how things should be; of what we should be entitled to; of how people should behave; of what is right and wrong.

In all of this we make very fine and detailed discriminations of how the world is, or what is appropriate, and under what circumstances.

Many of our judgements are based on stereotyped views that we pick up uncritically from those around us or from the wider culture in which we live. Many of our judgements we make out of habit, repeating the same pattern over and over again, without questioning what we are doing or whether we could see the world in another way.

Some of our most potent judgements are about other people. We frequently make these on the basis of scant information.

For example, we might make judgements about a person on the basis of how they speak, how they are dressed, how they look, their physical attributes, their gender, their nationality, or their race. These judgements are not infrequently loaded with strong emotion and have far reaching consequences for how we see the person, what we predict they are like, and how we subsequently relate to them.

Many readers will have had the experience that, although they do not regard themselves as a critical person, they sometimes feel tyrannised by the comparisons they make, and their judgements either of themselves or of other people. Many will also have had a sense of freedom when they let go and stop this intense judging and accept themselves or other people as they are. If you recognise this experience it will confirm for you how strongly our judging can affect our feelings.

Most of the time we operate somewhere between these two extremes of intensity of judging. We are then less aware that we are judging things, and it is harder for us to see how our judging influences our feelings; or to be more precise how our judging contains our feelings.

on judging:

"All things are less dreadful than they seem."
WORDSWORTH

"If you are pained by any external thing, it is not this thing that disturbs you, but your judgement about it. But it is in your power to wipe out this judgement."
MARCUS AURELIUS

"If you are quick to judge yourself, you may be slow to see the sentence you impose."
HOMER MALADROIT

CONCLUDING

The third aspect of our thinking that is important is that, on the basis of how we judge and compare things, we draw conclusions.

We are constantly trying to understand how the world is and our place in it. We make things matter in one way or another; we give meaning, importance and significance to things around us.

In the Decorated Room we use our judgements as evidence for a conclusion; ie, a thought that has wider implications than our judgements. We can then use this conclusion as the basis for bigger and bigger conclusions often based on small scraps of perception. We can draw a series of conclusions each bigger and more powerful than the last;-

	I haven't done a good job
therefore;	I am not a good decorator
therefore;	I am not a practical person
therefore;	I am no good as a person

In this hierarchy of conclusions the first is a conclusion about the whole room. The second extends this from our performance as a decorator on this one occasion to our skill as a decorator generally. The third extends the meaning from decorating to all practical skills. The fourth is a mega-conclusion about us as a person over all time, and all situations.

(It is not being suggested that we will necessarily be conscious of drawing such escalating conclusions; but, nevertheless, this is what we often do in the way we link ideas.)

We can see from this hierarchy that the further we go with our conclusions, the stronger our feelings are likely to be. We could stop our thinking at the thought "I haven't done a good job" Alternatively, we could go on to conclude that we are not good at anything. If we 'do' this bigger conclusion it clearly has within it bigger negative feelings.

Big conclusions bring big feelings.

A further important thing to note from the particular conclusions exemplified in the Decorated Room is the tendency we have to be preoccupied with evaluating ourselves. We want to know how good we are not just in our performance of a particular task on a particular occasion, but in general as a person. We want to know where we stand and how we measure up.

Perhaps, this tendency arises out of the fact that we are so judgmental, and yet there appears to be no objective, certain way that we can rely on to establish whether we have any worth. As a result we seek out apparent 'evidence', often in the slightest of details of our performance, our accomplishments, our acquisitions, our appearance, or others' reaction to us.

This preoccupation with our value leaves us frequently sensitive to criticism and likely to have an inflated response to success or flattery. It also leaves us open to forms of persuasion that carry the promise of securing our worth.

on concluding;

"Whether the event be cruel or kind,
it only matters how much we mind."
HOMER MALADROIT

"We do not discover the importance of any thing to us; we can only create it."
HOMER MALADROIT

"It does not matter, if you do not mind."
HOMER MALADROIT

THE NEW WAY OF UNDERSTANDING EXPERIENCE

We are constantly focusing, judging and concluding. These three aspects of our thinking make up the pathway that our thoughts take. Each of them is something we do inside our heads, and in each of them we are making choices that shape our experience. We usually make these choices without realising that we are doing anything. But they are choices nonetheless.

There is no rule book about what we should pay attention to. There is nothing fixed, or objective about how we should judge the things we focus on. There is nothing absolute or predetermined about what it means, or how much we should make it matter. There is simply no right view that we should hold. The issues at stake in each aspect of our thinking are essentially arbitrary and personal.

It is worth noting, in passing, that these three aspects of our thinking are not separate but frequently affect each other. For example the conclusions we draw have the potential to affect what we automatically focus on. If we make an imperfection matter, we are more likely to look for it the next time or to look for it in someone else's decorating. In the same way, a person can judge that their nose is not just big but too big. If they then conclude that this matters, they are likely to notice other people's noses before they focus on other things about them.

How we make things matter profoundly affects what we focus on. So the different aspects of our thinking (focusing, judging and concluding) are related in complex and subtle ways.

THE FALLACY OF IMMEDIACY

The Decorated Room suggests that all our experiences are constructed out of complex and detailed thinking.

We can think of this relationship between any experience and the thoughts that underlie it as roughly similar to the relationship that exists between the appearance of an object and the molecules out of which it is made.

When we look at an object we are not easily aware of how it is made; instead the visual appearance of an object has a strong sense of immediacy; a solidness and clarity.

In the same way, most of our experiences and feelings seem clear and natural, as if we are in touch with the very spirit of reality itself. They often seem indisputable, unquestionable; as if they could be no other way. This sense of immediacy can reinforce the impression that the source or cause of the experience is outside of us; and that the experience happens to us.

It is hard for us to be aware of the part our views, judgements and conclusions have played in making our experiences and feelings.

However, this sense of immediacy is an illusion. We take it as apparent confirmation that our feelings happen to us and are caused by the circumstances of our lives, but this is what could be called the fallacy of immediacy.

Whether it is a fallacy or not, it is probably the case that we value this sense of immediacy and often seek it. We want experiences that flow in this seamless and natural way. We like things to be spontaneous and effortless. Why should this be?

Perhaps, if reality seems immediate and clear, we as its viewers become clear and fixed by our connection with it. Perhaps, we then become free of doubt and ambiguity; free of the burden of responsibility of making arbitrary choices about values and options. Perhaps, it is for these reasons that immediacy seems so appealing.

On the other hand, some experiences do not seem immediate. They do not seem to flow comfortably; they can feel awkward, clumsy, unreal, laboured, even fake, alien, 'not us'.

When we adopt the new model of experience outlined by the Decorated Room we can understand how through our thinking we unwittingly construct our experience. We then have to conclude that a sense of immediacy simply arises when our thinking is operating in an unconscious, unquestioned way.

From this point of view some experiences that seem awkward can be seen in a new light. They are likely to occur when we do new, or unfamiliar things, or when we are changing old patterns of thinking and behaviour.

We can then see the sense of effort and clumsiness involved as intrinsic to this process of change or learning.

This sense of effort can be seen as something positive rather than something we do not want. It can be valued because of what we are trying to achieve.

IS THINKING INCIDENTAL OR CAUSATIVE?

Perhaps the most important conclusion that we must draw from the Decorated Room is that our view of the room is what determines our feelings as we sit in the room. Our feelings are not caused by the room or any aspects of it. What lies between the way the room is and how we feel as we sit there is what we are thinking at the time. Thinking matters.

If we feel frustrated when the job is done it is not because of the state of the room; it is because we are focusing on certain aspects and we are making these matter in a negative way; simultaneously we are ignoring other aspects and not appreciating or valuing them. In this way we are adopting a point of view or a stance. We need to understand that it is by doing these things that we determine our experience and feelings. Our feelings do not simply arise by themselves.

However, as I have already argued, when we talk about ourselves in everyday conversation we speak as if we are simply acted upon by events, circumstances and other people. When we do this we fail to recognise the importance of our thinking. We act as if our thinking is only incidental. As if it can be largely ignored. As if thinking is only a rational process that is determined by how things are in the world. As if thinking is the unambiguous result of us simply reflecting on how the world is. As if thinking is a passive process that changes nothing.

When we do this we are not recognising the power of our values, hopes and fears, and the way they run through our thoughts like the blood through our veins.

This is nothing short of a disaster for us. It has a number of deeply negative consequences that go to the heart of the quality of our lives, and our ability to understand and manage ourselves. It is through our hapless thinking that we create negativity, cynicism and unhappiness. It is through our hapless thinking that we fail to recognise opportunities, to foster appreciation and pleasure. It is through our hapless thinking that ultimately we trap ourselves in our psychological problems, whatever their form and intensity.

The Decorated Room offers us the argument, if not the proof, that our thinking is not merely incidental, it is causative. It is the means by which we unknowingly create our feelings and experience.

If we want to understand how we feel anything at all, we must pay attention to our thinking; what we focus on, how we predict, what we value, what we make important, how we judge and compare, what conclusions we draw, and what we want.

These are all personal acts that we commit. There is no rule book to guide us. Each involves personal choices. By committing them we are necessarily adopting a position in the world. Our ability to do this, or perhaps our inability not to do it, is perhaps the essence of what defines the human spirit.

In this sense thinking is an action in an inner world. The more evaluative this thinking the more this inner action will add emotion to our experience.

It is through the detail of this thinking, these acts within our heads, that we colour our world and animate ourselves.

But let me emphasise one thing for clarification. It is not that our thinking leads to our feelings. Thoughts and feelings are not different things. We should not think of thinking and emotion as different. The feelings we experience are contained in the evaluative thoughts we have. Feelings are evaluative thoughts. If we think "I am a bad person", and we do this with conviction, the bad feeling we feel is part of the thought; it cannot be separated from it.

CHOICE AND UNCONSCIOUSNESS
The Decorated Room shows us clearly that we have a whole host of choices regarding the view we take of any given situation. While we constantly make these choices at all sorts of levels in our thinking, we are hardly ever aware that we have a choice. We make the choices effortlessly and unconsciously.

We are largely unconscious creatures.

It is a matter of common observation that we are not conscious of how we do things and that we do not need to be. We are creatures of habit; by repeating a physical action over and over we can perform it with less effort and less conscious guidance until we can do it automatically.

The same is true of the choices we make in our thinking. With very little repetition they become established as habits.

Habits are immensely valuable; without them we could achieve very little. However, a downside of our facility to develop habits of thought is that once they are established they are very difficult to appreciate as acts that we have committed. It is not simply that habits are hard to break, it is more that we do not know that we are doing anything. We do not recognise that we are taking a position or operating from a particular perspective (with all of its inherent and arbitrary values).

We can become more aware of our habitual thinking simply by regarding it as important and by reflecting on it. We need to ask not "Why do I feel this?" but "How have I thought in order to feel it? What value-laden thoughts have I had that contain these feelings?"

To change a physical habit we usually have to work quite hard and repeat the new, more desired action until it becomes established as a habit.

Changing any age-old habit is often not easy. Recognising that we can make new choices today can overturn our approach to old situations and problems.

Changing habits of thought sometimes appears to be easier than changing physical habits. If we can identify a key idea or value that defines the new position we want to adopt, we can sometimes transform our thinking very quickly. But to overturn our approach to old situations and problems, we have to maintain the new thinking.

THINKING IS DYNAMIC

We usually expect each other to have categorical answers for questions such as; "Which do you prefer? Do you like your job? Are you in love? Who is your best friend? Is she right? Does he have a phobia?"

Underlying these questions there is an assumption that our thoughts are fairly simple, unambiguous and fixed or static.

But imagine you are sitting in your Decorated Room feeling somewhat frustrated because you are thinking negatively about it. A friend comes into the room. They are impressed. They make several complimentary comments about how good it looks and what a good job you have done.

You could ignore your friends comments and direct their attention to the room's imperfections. On the other hand if you allow your thoughts to follow your friend's you will immediately begin to feel better.

In practice, our view of our room will not remain fixed but can change frequently from negative to positive and back again. These changes can occur even from moment to moment and without any outside influence. By the time a period of weeks has elapsed we can sit in our room and pay it no attention at all; we do not notice it and, therefore, do not develop any pathway of thinking about it.

We do not simply think a view or position and hold to it from then on.

As our thoughts change, either from moment to moment or over longer periods, so do our feelings; our feelings are, after all, only contained in our thoughts.

The Decorated Room shows us that when we think we are doing something much more complex than we usually recognise. Our thoughts tumble after each other in a very complex way. The connections between one thought and the next are often highly individual and unpredictable. Our thinking will often not stay focused on one situation or issue but it can flow from one topic to another via a web of complex and personal meanings.

Often one view of a situation may even provoke awareness of another opposite view. We are not philosophers. We do not have the time to ensure that our thoughts are consistent and coherent (neither do we need to). As a result our thoughts and the feelings they contain often compete or contradict each other.

Thinking is a highly dynamic process. Our thoughts are constantly changing; ebbing and flowing; shifting, drifting, fading and flipping. We should recognise thinking as an ongoing, flowing and often restless process.

HERE-AND-NOW THINKING

We have become accustomed to thinking that our feelings, and particularly our difficulties, are determined by things that have happened in our past. These ideas have arisen partly from psychological theories that have proposed that we are determined by our early experiences and traumas. These ideas have become part of our everyday way of understanding ourselves.

In contrast to these ideas the Decorated Room shows that our present experiences are determined not by the past but by the way in which we are thinking now.

It is our here-and-now thinking, in all its active, ongoing, dynamic, flowing detail, that contains all of the complexity and richness of our present experience.

To appreciate this fully we need to have a full understanding of the complexity and detail of how we think. This is by no means an easy task as we enact so much of our thinking unconsciously, automatically by habit.

The emphasis on our here-and-now thinking does not mean that our past is unimportant. It is partly through past events, and the sense we have made and continue to make of them, that we draw ourselves into complex patterns of thinking. These patterns become so well established as habits that the choices we are making now, if not invisible to us, may seem to be utterly unchangeable.

However, much of our here-and-now thinking is also absorbed invisibly from our culture and those around us. Again we are usually unaware that we have been influenced and have adopted particular ideas or taken certain positions. (This very important source of influence is often not given much emphasis by those who believe we are determined by our individual pasts.)

Recognising that it can only be our here-and-now thinking that drives our current experience can, with practice, help us find new ways of thinking. This can free us from some of the thinking that we have built up from our pasts and our culture.

MOOD

In real life we are often not simply concerned with how we react to a single situation such as a Decorated Room. On the contrary, we recognise that we can spend long periods of time in a particular frame of mind or mood that seems to spread out across time and over most situations we come into contact with. Such moods will not only influence the views we take of our current situation but they will also affect our remembering of events and our anticipation of future ones.

Is the Decorated Room too simple to give us an account of our complexity? Can it offer a way of understanding moods and how they work?

Let us return to the Room. Suppose you have developed a positive view of the room and have drawn a limited positive conclusion that a certain part of it has been done well. If you do not draw any larger positive conclusions than this, when you get up and leave the room, this positive conclusion will not have any particular relevance to the next situation you come across. The positive view is, therefore, not likely to influence the view you take of the next situation, and so your frame of mind does not necessarily endure or gather momentum.

On the other hand, if you have developed bigger, positive conclusions, perhaps, even as far as "everything I do turns out well" or "I am pretty good", then when you leave the room these conclusions are much more likely to have relevance to the next situation you find yourself in. You are then more likely to take a view of the next situation that fits in with these big, positive conclusions. Your frame of mind will then be prolonged or even gather pace.

From this we can see that the bigger the conclusions we draw, not only do they have more emotional power, but they also apply to a wider range of situations. In this way we can see that broad conclusions have power to bring about moods, good and bad.

However, we must remind ourselves that we can only stay in a particular frame of mind or mood while we persist in seeing things from that perspective. It is a frame of mind that we are actively, but usually unwittingly, engaged in nurturing and developing. One way we do this is by selecting particular things to focus on. We can do this not just with present situations but with the past and future. We can choose to remember good or bad things; we can select future events to be apprehensive about or ones to look forward to.

A mood can only endure as long as we continue the type of thinking that lies behind it.

A mood is not something outside us that is acting upon us; it is us unwittingly continuing to act from a particular viewpoint or value-laden position.

FACT AND VALUE

Over recent centuries we have come to emphasise our rationality. This is partly because of the very obvious success of rational thinking that underpins the spectacular advances in science and technology. This has, perhaps, seduced us into thinking that we are just rational, or that our aim should be to be as rational as we can.

What this blinds us to is the simple fact that we are mostly unconscious creatures, and that much of our thinking is value-based, personal, subjective and arbitrary; it is concerned with our tastes, our attachments and our intentions.

Facts are at least theoretically value-free. The universe does not mind. While we are forced to adapt to its structures and limits, it does not determine how we should judge or evaluate things.

Within very broad ranges we are free to like and dislike, to want and to fear, to make things matter and to form attachments to people, places, activities and things. We do so with great variety and in the finest of detail.

In the way we have thought about ourselves in the recent past, we have not recognised the importance of our value-based thinking and how it will always be the source of all of our feelings.

on appreciation:

"Appreciation adds sweetness to any moment."
HOMER MALADROIT

"Whatever the goods of fortune are, a man must have a proper sense to favour them. It is the enjoying, and not the possessing of them that makes us happy."
MONTAIGNE

"Without earnestness there is nothing to be done in life."
GOETHE

HOW USEFUL IS THE DECORATED ROOM?
We can use the ideas of the Decorated Room as a tool to understand all of our thinking about the situations in our daily lives; and more broadly our ideas about ourselves and the issues and challenges we face. It can help us understand our passions as well as our problems.

For example, it gives us a way of understanding how we think about ourselves; our self-confidence and our self-esteem. The Decorated Room tells us that we should think about these things as things we "do" not as things we "have".

Another area where the Decorated Room leads to new insights is in the understanding and overcoming of psychological problems. This includes problems that many would call psychiatric or mental health problems; eg, the many varieties of anxiety and depression.

These problems usually arise because the person has one or more complex issues in their lives. These issues matter to the person, but they fail to recognise the intensity, complexity and often the contradictory nature of their thinking about the issues. The intensity of their thinking gives rise to a variety of sensations and emotions.

As the source of these feelings and sensations is not recognised, the feelings and sensations are often experienced as coming 'out of the blue'. The person then focuses on these sensations and feelings, and is naturally concerned about them; they frequently judge them to be unwanted, unhealthy or abnormal.

(Our problems are fundamentally underpinned by our ideas about what is normal. In general we have restricted expectations about what we should feel and these ideas form an important background from which we judge challenging and novel experiences.)

The individual wants to make sense of the sensations and feelings. They want to know why they occur, when they will happen again, and how bad they might become. The individual's best guess is that they must arise through illness, neurosis or imminent madness; and that they are likely to lead to social or physical disaster.

The person is then alarmed by their own thinking about these possibilities. They develop an inward concern with themselves and their experience that extends and intensifies their bad feelings. Not unnaturally, they want to protect themselves. They often blame their feelings on the situation in which they occur and adopt various precautions and avoidance behaviour. They frequently want to hide what they feel is happening to them, thus adding shame to the constellation of their emotions.

When we react in this manner we are using what I have called the old models of experience. These are the models mainly available in our culture; with them we succeed only in intensifying our problems.

We can see from this extremely brief description that the person with the problem is actively engaged in focusing, judging and concluding in very intense ways. This is the source of our psychological problems and how we unwittingly create them.

on the possibility of changing our thoughts;

"When we want to gain new insight, it must be our first concern to make us free from old prejudiced opinion."
FRANCIS BACON.

"I am the drug."
SALVADOR DALI

"I am my choices."
SARTRE

"It is often better not to see an insult than to avenge it."
SENECA

"Thought is too wayward to be controlled by reason."
HOMER MALADROIT

"Everything that is worth thinking has been thought before; we must only try to think it again."
GOETHE

THE NEED FOR CHANGE

At first sight it might not be apparent that when we talk about our feelings in everyday conversation we are making a number of assumptions about the nature of our experience.

These assumptions are hidden from our view by their very familiarity. However, they lie just beneath the surface of the words and phrases we use in our descriptions. Therefore, only a little study is necessary to reveal the models we are using to describe and explain our experience.

We speak of 'having' no confidence, 'falling in' love and 'bottling up' our feelings; we speak of 'suffering' from depression, anxiety and post traumatic stress; we speak of people, events and circumstances 'making' us feel this or that emotion; we speak of feeling 'with' our hearts, having 'gut' feelings and feeling it 'in our bones'.

These expressions use a number of different models. They are not clearly defined or distinct. Sometimes they are at odds with each other, but the models that we most widely use tend to share common themes.

Most of the time we describe ourselves as relatively passive victims of our situations and circumstances, our biology and our biography.

This is not merely a matter of interest to academics and people who want to study such issues. It is a matter of vital importance to us all.

The way in which each of us describes how experience works, shapes the quality of our individual experiences and feelings. It shapes fundamentally who we think we are, and what we believe is possible. It determines to a large extent how much control we have over our lives.

It also has consequences for our understanding of human nature itself. It will be a basis for how we regard and treat other people. It will be part of the social fabric; a foundation stone of our culture.

The Decorated Room offers a very different way of thinking about experience; by highlighting the importance of the flow of our thoughts, it suggests that we are not passive victims but active agents who are constantly making choices and taking positions.

For many people the appeal of the Decorated Room is that it is obvious. Once it is described we can recognise that it captures how our thinking operates.

Like many revelations, it works because it seems to explain what we have already sensed, at least to some degree, and on some occasions. However, while we might be able to recognise its value, it is not a body of ideas that we are used to using consistently. Furthermore, it is not necessarily easy to appreciate how different the ideas are from those that we currently use.

Given the usefulness of the Decorated Room, it would be incomprehensible for its principles not to be already woven into our culture in many implicit ways. What the Decorated Room offers is a memorable way of drawing these strands of recognition together and making them explicit and coherent. Without such an example our intuitive understanding of the issues tends to remain fragmentary, and easily overwhelmed by competing understandings.

The example of the Decorated Room, therefore, allows us to harness this way of understanding experience; we are then more able to use it systematically should we wish to.

The ideas put forward in this book are at the same time simple and profound. They lead to exciting possibilities for understanding our experience in new ways with the prospect of overcoming difficulties and increasing our appreciation and pleasures..

We, individually and collectively, need to learn to operate with the model of experience revealed by the Decorated Room.

We need to learn to apply it to the detail of our lives as we see fit.

We need to have a fuller appreciation of how complex and sophisticated we are as human beings.

We need to recognise the central, driving force of our thinking in creating our experience and feelings; that the range of our feelings from passion to terror arises from the detail of our here-and-now thinking.

We need to see that we are constantly interpreting the world and that our thoughts are laced with our personal values and points of view.

We need to recognise how fluid and dynamic our thinking is.

We need to overcome our narrow ideas of the range of feelings (and their physical aspects) that we might experience; and recognise the universality and, therefore, the normality of a much wider range of feelings than we presently do.

We need to review our ways of explaining why we should experience unexpected or novel or intense feelings; and to move away from judging them as abnormal, and away from explanations that see them as arising because of illness or mental breakdown.

We need to recognise that the cause of experience is the detail and complexity of how we are thinking at the time and that this explanation is very different from blaming external factors (events, circumstances, trauma) or internal fixed qualities (personality, inherited characteristics, biochemistry).

Ultimately these ideas need to become part of our culture. By definition, this will only be achieved when a sufficient number of people use the model and support each other's use of it. Only then would its real potential be realised.

on the need for cultural change in our understanding of thinking;

"No great improvements in the lot of mankind are possible, until a great change takes place in the fundamental constitution of their modes of thought."
JOHN STUART MILL

However, even without wider cultural change individuals can use the ideas of the Decorated Room to enhance their lives and to understand and overcome their psychological problems.

We should start by seeing these problems not as illnesses or neuroses, but as arising from an intent and sincere attempt to understand our predicaments. An intent and sincere, but nonetheless, unhelpful attempt that ends with us being entangled in a way of seeing the world that is negative and self-defeating. The ideas in this book offer a radical alternative and with them we can overcome our problems and sometimes literally transform our lives.

We must first achieve a thorough understanding of how experience works. Secondly, we must develop our appreciation of the detail and dynamics of our own thinking. Thirdly, we need to see how we have unwittingly created our 'problem' thinking; (usually we will have focused on feelings, judged them as bad, made catastrophic predictions, tried to escape and avoid them, and on top of all this we will have felt bad about ourselves for having a problem.) When we have achieved this awareness, we can begin to patiently overcome our problems systematically by learning to think differently.

In a similar way, we can use the ideas from the Decorated Room, to enrich our lives by nurturing our appreciation and our wanting; over time we can take a more active and conscious part in building and maintaining our attachments and passions; ie, those things which give our lives depth and meaning.

CONCLUSION

This book has argued that our current way of thinking about how our feelings arise is unhelpful in a number of important ways. By seeing ourselves as pushed and pulled by the situations and circumstances of our lives, and by explaining our reactions in terms of our personality, biological make-up or our early experiences, we paint a portrait of ourselves as essentially passive victims.

In doing so we fail to see how we really operate in the world. We fail to see our richness, and complexity. We fix ourselves unnecessarily and we underestimate our degrees of choice and, therefore, our freedom.

The Decorated Room leads to a new way of understanding how experience works. It suggests the simple rule that if we want to understand our feelings at any point in time we should pay attention to our thinking at that time.

Thinking is not merely incidental; it is an on-going, active, expressive, creative process. It is our thinking that drives our experience and feelings.

However, we must respect that we are largely unconscious creatures. All of our waking time we are thinking, and our thoughts are constantly changing. These thoughts are laced with our values. They are views about how we would like the world to be. They are thoughts that assert our likes and dislikes; that nurture and breathe life into our pleasures and attachments, as well as our displeasure and our hatreds.

They are views that adopt perspectives or positions; that contain all sorts of focusing, judging and concluding; all sorts of hopes/fears, memories/predictions.

It is by choosing these value-laden positions that we colour our world, and animate, not only ourselves but each of our moments. Without value-based thinking our lives would be colourless and meaningless.

It is by our here-and-now thinking in all its richness and complexity that we unwittingly, (sometimes recklessly, and frequently just out of habit), create our experience of the moment. We are the secret agent of our own experience.

The Decorated Room should not be mistaken only for an argument for positive thinking. It should not be read as an argument that we should not have negative feelings. It does not suggest that we should be calm and rational at all times. The complexity, detail, unconsciousness and dynamic nature of thinking means that we can only ever be like this for brief periods.

While we can have considerable influence on our thinking we should not expect to control it.

Furthermore, the Decorated Room does not tell us anything about how we should live; what values, morals, aims and ambitions we should adopt. The latter are our individual responsibility; they are our choice.

The Decorated Room also allows us to see that the differences between people do not need to be explained in terms of their different biographies and biologies. Instead, we can see that two people will have different experiences in the same situation simply because they are thinking or operating differently at the time.

Similarly, an individual will have a different experience of the same situation on different occasions, if, and only if, they think differently on the two occasions.

Lastly, the Decorated Room allows us to re-think psychological problems. We can see them, not as illnesses or breakdowns, but as misguided attempts to understand our reactions; as unfortunate ways of thinking that we build up over time.

Our 'problem' thinking is usually characterised by an inner focus and a major concern with what is happening to us; we unwittingly become preoccupied with ourselves and come to believe that something awful is happening to us.

Overall, the ideas of the Decorated Room suggest a new direction for us if we want to manage our lives more effectively. Understanding these ideas is not enough; we have to give ourselves time to patiently apply them to the detail of our lives.

ALSO PUBLISHED BY MINDS EYE BOOKS

RELAXATION RULES
A practical guide to understanding tension and relaxation. It gives a detailed framework for becoming more aware of physical tension and suggests practical ideas on what to do about it. Tension is an ordinary part of our everyday lives; but there is more to relaxation than doing relaxing things at the end of the day. The booklet shows you how to be more relaxed throughout the day whatever you are doing.

WORKING AT REDUNDANCY
A guide to understanding the experience of redundancy. It does not deal with the practical tasks of writing CVs and job hunting; it outlines the sort of reactions people go through from shock and disbelief, through anger, to acceptance. It shows how redundancy can challenge our everyday thoughts and beliefs. By explaining redundancy as a process that involves rethinking and adjustment it gives the reader a framework to deal with it more positively.

It has been used by many organisations including Marconi, Plessey, John Brown Engineers, Ferranti, The Marketing Society and the University of Portsmouth.

COMMON PSYCHOLOGICAL PROBLEMS
Using real life-stories, this booklet shows how psychological problems arise because we misunderstand aspects of our lives. This leads on to unsuccessful attempts at solving unhappiness. The booklet shows how a straightforward cognitive psychological approach begins by offering more constructive ways of describing the problems, and how this leads naturally to better solutions.

HOMER MALADROIT'S GUIDE TO ANALYSING PSYCHOLOGISTS

This illustrated booklet suggests that Clinical Psychologists are not doctors, healers, magicians, mind readers, absolvers, observers or advisers. They do not measure personality, read the unconscious mind, sympathise, protect, or know what's best.

Psychologists act like coaches. The latter understand the complexities and issues of skills and can give feedback and support to help individuals improve their performance. Similarly Psychologists, through listening and discussion, help individuals make sense of their experiences in new ways that lead to the recognition of new possibilities and choices.

RELAX AND ENJOY IT
A relaxation tape by Dr. R Sharpe

For up to date prices send a stamped, addressed envelope to :-

MINDS EYE BOOKS
16 HELENA ROAD
SOUTHSEA
HANTS
PO4 9RH

TELE;- (023) 9283 1457

Or e-mail; ChristinaMerrett@hotmail.com